CW00350813

THE COMPLETE COCKTAIL MAKER

The COMPLETE COCKTAIL MAKER

Geoffrey Hindley

Ebury Press · London

Published by Ebury Press
National Magazine House
72 Broadwick Street
London W1V 2BP

First impression 1983

ISBN 0 85223 335 3

Designed by Bob Hall

Illustrations by Carlotta Barrow

Photographs: Paul Kemp, facing pages 17, 32, 81;
Paul Williams, facing pages 16, 33, 64, 65.

Typeset by MS Filmsetting Limited, Frome, Somerset
Printed and bound by New Interlitho s.p.a. Milan

Contents

Introduction

This is an entirely new kind of cocktail book. If you have any booze in the cupboard and a reasonably well-stocked fridge you should be able to begin the cocktail adventure now, without the purchase of a single extra bottle and without the chore of searching the index to find a recipe matching the ingredients actually to hand.

The book aims to explore and expand the possibilities of the drinks cupboard on a planned buying programme and with the help of a series of charts. The first is what one may call the Basic Cupboard (see page 15) of the familiar spirits, aperitifs and fortified wines such as port and sherry. After all, if you have none of these bottles, you are unlikely to have bought the book. If you have more than one, you will probably find you can already mix your first cocktail. Later chapters introduce a variety of the liqueurs, most with their own charts, showing at a glance the range of cocktails you can make with each one. This book takes your present drinks cupboard as its starting point and shows how with the purchase of any one new bottle your horizons immediately extend.

Furthermore, you will discover the basic principles behind the mixing of drinks. It is reckoned that more than 7,000 cocktail recipes have been published over the past century. With the aid of this book—and an earnest-minded desire for self-improvement—you should be able to learn the essentials of the art and so add a few classics of your own to the number. Happy drinking!

The Story of the Cocktail

Cocktails and bootleggers, whatever the pundits may say, are two sides of the same coin. Sober history, or what passes for such, tells us that the word 'cocktail' is first found in an American journal of the year 1806 and it was certainly known to the cad Flashman of *Tom Brown's Schooldays*. But for all that, it was the America of the Twenties and Thirties, the America of the flapper, the Great Gatsby and Prohibition which witnessed the first Cocktail Age. Recipes for mixed drinks multiplied then as research pressed forward into ways of making bath-tub gin and bootleg hooch palatable. Today, when the glorious mirrored cocktail cabinets of those decades are being auctioned off to collectors, a second Cocktail Age is under way.

But why 'cocktail'? The derivations given for the name are almost as diverse as the recipes it describes. One line of thinking holds that it refers in some way to the actual tail of the cock— possibly a kind of toast to a victorious fighting cock, possibly a drinks' stirrer decorated with or looking like a cock's tail feather. Another school of thought claims the word to be a corruption of the French '*coquetel*', a wine cup from the Bordeaux region, perhaps mixed for French sailors on the waterfront of New Orleans and picked up by English and American seamen. According to what we might call the mythological theory, the first cocktail was served by Coctel, Princess of Mexico and daughter of King Axolotl to an American ship's company 'sometime about the beginning of the last century', a delightful picture marred only slightly by the fact that the last 'king' of Mexico had been overthrown by the Spaniards some three centuries earlier. What the actual derivation may have been I doubt will ever be known. Perhaps it is best to leave the question in the no doubt lovely, if legendary, hands of Princess Coctel.

Mixed drinks as such are probably as old as drink itself. They were certainly known to the ancient Greeks who used a mixing bowl which they called a *krater*. The fact that we use that word for the crater of a volcano seems to me to be somehow significant! The Romans thought that truth lay in wine—*in vino veritas*—and people were still busily mixing drinks in medieval Europe. As in Greece and Rome, the principal ingredients were wine, herbs and spices and the result, taken for strictly medicinal purposes you understand, was named, *hippocras*, after the great physician Hippocrates. Honey played an important role in these medieval recipes but it was gradually displaced by sugar. The men and women of Shakespeare's England were known throughout Europe for their passion for mixed drinks of wine and sugar. The habit no doubt developed in part as a defence against the quality of the basic liquor—anticipating by several centuries the principle of the Prohibition cocktail. In those times, wine was drunk young, rarely travelled well and had little of the sophistication of the great vintages of later centuries.

The hot punches of today are the descendants of such concoctions. **Negus**, for example, dates back at least to the seventeenth century. A modern recipe calls for one bottle of sherry, two pints of boiling water, a lemon, a wine glass of brandy, sugar, nutmeg and cloves. Mulled ale has a still more venerable ancestry, but that is another story.

When gin arrived in England from Holland in the seventeenth century, the English had something else to mix with their beloved sugar. The result was the **Sling**. Sometimes thought to be an American invention, it was, as we know from the *Rural Rides* of William Cobbett, certainly being served in the George Inn, Andover, Wiltshire, England, as early as 1825. The **Cobbler**, a simple drink of one liquor with sugar served with a straw in a glass of crushed ice, probably is of American origin. Dickens's hero Martin Chuzzlewit drank his first **Sherry Cobbler** during his ill-fated adventures in the United States.

According to one American barman of the 1880s the **Cobbler** was then 'the most popular beverage in the country with ladies as well as gentlemen'. By this time the world's first cocktail book was some twenty years old. Published in 1862 by the American bartender Jerry Thomas, *The Bon Vivant's Guide* was subtitled *How to Mix Drinks*. London's first cocktail bar was probably the American Bar opened in 1910. Many books and hundreds of bars later let us now turn our attention to the sociable and satisfying business of mixing cocktails in the home.

The Making of the Cocktail

ICE

- The colder you can regulate the freezer compartment the better—this way you will cool your drinks more even before the ice begins to melt.

- The ideal is clean translucent ice. Keep the freezer compartment clean and regularly defrosted; the chlorine and purifying chemicals in tap water tend to cloud the ice so it is worth trying bottled spring water. Use ice only direct from the freezer or from the ice bucket, and ideally you should not re-use ice in the shaker.

- The larger the surface area of ice brought into contact with the liquor, the quicker it will be cooled, so the smaller the compartments in your ice tray the better. Crushed ice is best produced with an ice crusher but these come expensive. Hammer the cubes in a tea towel with a kitchen mallet but do not use the smallest slivers in the shaker as these melt very quickly.

- Virtually every known cocktail is mixed on ice either in the shaker or the mixing jug—*use plenty of it.*

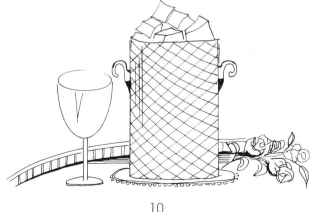

MIXING METHOD

- **Chill** the shaker and glasses beforehand if there is room in the fridge. Alternatively, top up the glasses with crushed ice while mixing the drink.

- **Put** the ice into your shaker or mixing jug first.

- **Pour** non-alcoholic ingredients first.

- **Shake** when the recipe includes fruit juices, eggs, cream, etc. with a sharp, vigorous action but not for too long.

- **Stir** when all the ingredients are clear, as shaking would tend to cloud them, as does too-energetic stirring.

- **Blend** when the recipe specifies. Drinks' blenders are expensive, but if you use a standard kitchen blender be sure to crush the ice well, if this is to be blended with the other ingredients, to safeguard the blades of the blender.

MEASURING

Even classic recipes differ from barman to barman and from book to book, reflecting the judgement of the individual and it is worth taking some trouble about consistent measuring. Once you are surehanded with proportions, you will be able to modify them and devise new recipes certain that any happy discovery can be repeated.

A standard cocktail measure is the jigger of $1\frac{1}{2}$ fluid ounces or 40 millilitres, a little under a pub double and roughly equivalent to two tablespoonsful. Measures of various sizes can be bought but, as one recent book observes, even the standard egg cup will serve so long as you know its capacity and use it consistently. The simplest utensil is a graduated measuring beaker.

Most of the recipes in this book are given in proportions—the actual quantities of each main ingredient depending on the number of drinks required. To start with, the easiest way to make up small numbers is to use that medicinal measuring beaker with its millilitre graduations. A standard 4-oz cocktail glass holds just over 112 ml (1 fluid oz = 28.4 ml). If you are making two drinks of a recipe requiring, let us say, five main parts, then simple arithmetic shows that you need about 225 ml in total or, divided by 5, 45 ml of each part. After some basic experimentation along these lines, you will soon be mixing your favourite cocktails 'by eye'.

A barspoon has the same capacity as a teaspoon. The dash is an indeterminate small measure but a rough guide gives four dashes to the barspoon. Where the dash or barspoon features in a recipe that quantity is needed for each of the drinks to be mixed. In those recipes where there could have been any confusion about proportions, we have stated the number of barspoons or dashes needed for each individual drink.

EQUIPMENT

You can mix cocktails in a wide-necked jar with a screw cap as a shaker, using a large kitchen strainer to hold back the ice. But a three-piece shaker with built-in strainer is simpler to use and more fun. In addition you will need:

- A large mixing glass or jug, with

- A long-handled barspoon for stirring and measuring (a glass stirring rod and a teaspoon will serve the two functions equally well).

- A bar strainer or a 'hawthorne' strainer.

I assume you already have corkscrew, bottle opener, fruit squeezer, sharp fruit knife and chopping board. There is plenty of other more extravagant apparatus—for instance, the Boston shaker consisting of two cones, one of glass the other of metal— but if you have everything on the above list, you are well equipped to start making cocktails.

GLASS

Fine quality clear glass so enhances the quality of the presentation of your drinks that it is worth getting the best you can. Keep it clean, rinse it thoroughly when washing up and dry and polish it with a lint-free glass cloth. There are many types of glass available, some of which are illustrated opposite page 16.

- Cocktail glass: 3 to 4 ounce capacity.

- Tall straight-sided tumbler: 8 to 12 ounce capacity, commonly called a 'highball' glass.

- Wine glasses of 4, 6 and 8 ounce capacity.

- Whisky tumbler of 8 ounce capacity commonly called an 'old-fashioned' glass.

The Basic Cupboard

Take a look at the chart overleaf to see which you have of the ingredients listed in its headings. The most common spirits are listed down the left-hand side—American whiskey and tequila have their own sections at the end of the book and are not included here. Two of the spirits are repeated at the head of the chart as they are combined with other spirits in a few recipes. The rest of the top line is occupied by the fortified wines, sherry and port; vermouth and the aperitif wines—Dubonnet, Campari, St. Raphael and so forth come under this heading; and a column of recipes headed 'Extras'. Check your cupboard to find which drinks you have. To find the cocktails you can make with them, read across and down to find the answer in the box. This refers you to the alphabetical list of recipes, where you will find any 'Extras' that may be required besides those alcoholic ingredients already indicated in the chart. If you have only whisky and rum there is no cocktail for you—though vodka and rum is another matter (see **Intrepid**). The chart, in other words, is used like a road mileage chart.

There is one other set of ingredients besides alcohol, that you will need and these are covered by the end column 'Extras'. This has cocktails, short and long, which require only one alcoholic part and those needing any of the following as major ingredients:

- **Fruit juices** Squeeze fruit juices fresh whenever possible and strain through a fine mesh (i.e. tea) strainer if you can bear the trouble.

- **Eggs and cream** Check you have these in the fridge.

- **Sugar** If used in the solid state, powdered or icing sugar is best. However, **sugar syrup**, called by bartenders 'gomme' (pronounced 'gum') syrup, is easy to make and worth ten minutes of your time. Dissolve one pound of ordinary granulated sugar and a teaspoon of glucose in half a pint of hot water, stirring in enough cold water to bring up to the pint. Boil for five minutes and, when cool, store in the fridge in an air-tight container where it will keep for a month.

- **Mixers** I assume you have the usual mixers, such as tonic, soda and ginger ale, but in addition I recommend a few cans of ginger beer (Idris I reckon the best).

- **Bitters** You should acquire a bottle of bitters at the earliest opportunity. The most commonly used are Angostura bitters and even a small bottle goes a long way as few recipes call for more than two or three dashes. If you can get them, orange bitters, less concentrated and less bitter, are a delicate flavouring agent. Peach bitters are another fruit-flavoured type. If you have only Angostura to hand and the recipe specifies orange, use a smaller quantity. However, for these recipes the orange bitters are worth the search.

- **Fruit syrups** There are numerous types—orgeat for example, has a subtle almond flavour. However, grenadine, non-alcoholic and flavoured with pomegranate, is the most common one and occurs in many recipes. Coconut cream, with or without rum, is now widely available for **Pina Colada.**

- **Decoration** Fruits of various kinds, cocktail cherries, olives, cocktail onions and spices such as cinnamon and nutmeg, are often required for decoration, so keep up your stocks. 'A twist of lemon peel' should be peeled without pith, twisted over the drink to release the oils and then dropped into the glass.

- **Ice** Finally remember that, except for a handful of cases, all the recipes in this book are to be mixed, shaken or stirred with ice.

	Rum	Brandy	Aperitif/ * Vermouth	Sherry/Port	Extras
Gin	Junior Judge Morro's	London Highball Dubonnet Negroni Salome		Rupert	Clover Club Gimlet Gin and Sin Shady Grove
Whisky				Thunderstick	Mamie Taylor Scotch Sour
Vodka	Intrepid	Kutusov		Sherryade	Bloody Mary Russet Salty Dog Screwdriver
Rum		Margaret Mine	Bushranger	Quarter Deck	Bacardi Nevada Pineapple Simple Planter's Punch
Brandy			Montana Cocktail Coffee Portwine Cocktail		Brandy Gump Brandy Sangaree Brandy Sour Prairie Oyster

BACARDI

See Daiquiri, Classics page 33

BLOODY MARY

See Classics page 32

*The cocktails that have vermouth as a principal ingredient are so numerous that they have their own specific section, pages 22–28.

BRANDY GUMP

1 part brandy ● 1 part lemon juice ● 2 or 3 dashes grenadine

Shake.

BRANDY SANGAREE

See *Sangaree, Classics* page 37

BRANDY SOUR

1½ ounces brandy ● juice of ½ lemon ● ½ barspoon powdered sugar

Shake and strain into a whisky glass and decorate with half a slice of lemon and a cherry. As with all **Sours** the proportions of 'sweet', 'sour' and 'strong' are matters of personal taste.

BUSHRANGER

3 parts white rum ● 2 parts Dubonnet ● 2 dashes bitters per drink

Stir.

CLOVER CLUB

See *Classics* page 32

COFFEE COCKTAIL

1 part brandy ● 1 part port

1 barspoon sugar syrup ● 1 egg per two drinks

Shake, strain and decorate with a sprinkle of nutmeg. You may prefer to use only the yolk of the egg. A dash of curacao gives a touch of luxury, too. The drink is named for its colour rather than its contents—it is especially pleasant with an after dinner coffee.

DUBONNET

1 part gin ● 1 part Dubonnet ● 1 dash bitters (optional)

Stir and add twist of lemon.

Top shelf: whisky (old fashioned) tumbler; assorted bar measures; pourer; small whisky tumbler or tot.

Middle shelf: tall tumbler (highball glass); double cocktail glass; standard cocktail glass; saucer champagne glass; tumbler (highball glass); three-piece cocktail shaker; Boston shaker, top and bottom.

Bottom shelf: champagne flute; 4-ounce wine glass; mixing glass with barspoon and muddler; manual ice crusher; ice bucket with tongs.

Foreground: bar strainer – a 'Hawthorne' strainer is similar but does not have the two projecting lugs; fruit knife; straws.

Dry Martini (left); Sweet Martini.

GIMLET

See *Classics* page 34

GIN AND SIN

2 parts gin • 2 parts lemon juice

1 part orange juice • 1 dash grenadine per drink

Shake.

INTREPID

3 parts vodka • 1 part white rum • 1 part lime juice or lemon juice

1 or 2 dashes powdered sugar per drink

Shake. Decorate with slice of lime or lemon.

JUNIOR JUDGE

2 parts gin • 2 parts dark rum • 1 part lemon juice

1 barspoon grenadine per drink • 1 dash powdered sugar per drink

(optional)

Shake.

KUTUSOV

1 part brandy • 1 part vodka

Stir without ice and serve in a small whisky glass. For the related **Barclay de Tolly**, substitute whisky for the brandy and stir with or without ice.

LONDON HIGHBALL

1 part gin • 1 part brandy • 1 part sweet vermouth

1 dash bitters (orange for preference) • ginger ale

Shake. Pour over ice into an ice-filled tall glass and top up with the ginger ale.

MAMIE TAYLOR

3 ounces whisky ● juice of $\frac{1}{4}$ lemon or $\frac{1}{2}$ lime ● ginger ale

Squeeze the juice into a tall glass, add two or three lumps of ice, pour in the whisky (2 ounces if you prefer a weaker drink) and top up with ginger ale. Add the fruit wedge.

MARGARET MINE

2 parts golden rum ● 1 part brandy ● 2 barspoons lemon juice

2 barspoons orange juice ● 1 dash grenadine

Shake. You could give this a try with white rum.

MONTANA

3 parts brandy ● 1 part dry vermouth ● 2 parts port

Pour over ice cubes in a small tumbler and stir. An English version of this American recipe varies the proportions somewhat and calls in addition for 1 or 2 dashes each of Angostura bitters and anisette per drink.

MORRO'S

2 parts gin ● 1 part dark rum ● 1 part pineapple juice

1 part lime or lemon juice ● 1 barspoon powdered sugar per drink

Moisten the rim of a chilled wine glass with lime or lemon and twirl in a saucer of sugar. Shake and strain. Decorate with a small wedge of pineapple.

NEGRONI

1 part gin ● 1 part sweet vermouth

1 part Campari ● soda water (optional)

Stir and pour into a cocktail glass or over ice cubes in a tumbler if you like your **Negronis** topped up with soda. Decorate with orange rind. Some prefer a higher proportion of gin.

NEVADA

3 parts white rum ● 2 parts grapefruit juice

1 part lime juice ● 2 barspoons sugar syrup per drink

Shake. If you use lemon instead of lime juice, reduce the amount of sugar syrup.

PINEAPPLE SIMPLE

2 parts white rum ● 1 part pineapple juice

2 dashes lemon juice ● 1 dash sugar syrup

Shake and serve with a cherry.

PLANTER'S PUNCH

Some would say this should be with the classics and there are many different recipes.

2 or 3 parts dark rum ● 1 part lime or lemon juice

1 barspoon grenadine or 2 barspoons sugar

1 dash Angostura bitters ● soda water

Fill a tall glass with crushed ice, pour in the ingredients and stir. Top up with soda water and decorate with slices of orange and lemon—a pineapple slice and cherry, too, if you wish. A sprig of mint frosted with castor sugar is a nice touch—this is one drink where you need not fear the despised 'fruit salad' effect. Serve with straws.

PORTWINE COCKTAIL

4 parts brandy ● 1 part port

Stir with or without ice. Decorate with twist of orange peel.

PRAIRIE OYSTER (BRANDY)

A healthy variant of the classic pick-me-up on page 36 to which you add an ounce or so of brandy.

QUARTER DECK

2 parts dark rum ● 1 part sherry

1 barspoon lime juice or a dash of lime cordial/juice

Shake or, with the cordial, stir. An invigorating old version of this recipe comprises: 2 rum, 1 dry sherry; 1 whisky; with a dash of orange bitters and powdered sugar.

RUPERT

2 parts gin ● 1 part sherry ● 1 part cream

Shake, strain into a cocktail glass and dust with nutmeg.

RUSSET

1 part vodka ● 1 part apple juice

1 barspoon lemon juice ● 1 barspoon grenadine

Shake.

SALOME

1 part gin ● 1 part dry vermouth ● 1 part Dubonnet

Stir.

SALTY DOG

1 part vodka ● 2 parts grapefruit juice ● salt to taste

Pour the ingredients over ice cubes (increase the proportion of vodka if you prefer) and stir in the salt. This is as good as a glass of grappa for clearing the head after a heavy drinking session. Technically, the salt should be 'frosted' round the moistened rim of the glass and the liquid drunk through it.

SCOTCH SOUR

A variation of the classic **Whiskey Sour** on page 37

SCREWDRIVER

See *Classics* page 37

SHADY GROVE

3 parts gin • 1 part lemon juice

1 barspoon powdered sugar per drink • ginger beer

Shake, strain over ice in a tall glass and top up with (Idris) ginger beer. Decorate with a wedge of lemon.

SHERRYADE

1 part vodka • 1 part sherry • 1 barspoon lemon juice

1 barspoon orange juice • sugar syrup to taste

Shake.

THUNDERSTICK

1 part whisky • 1 part sherry (medium or dry)

1 barspoon orange juice per drink • 1 barspoon lemon juice per drink

sugar syrup to taste

Shake.

The Vermouth Constellation

Vermouth was being used in cocktails as early as 1860. The most famous of them all, the **Martini** has its own section, but this chapter presents a selection from the other stars in this vast constellation.

Vermouth is compounded of a wine base, aromatic herbs and spices, sugar and additional alcohol, such as brandy. The process is elaborate and the recipes are closely guarded secrets. Herbs were being infused in wine, both as a preservative and for medicinal purposes, in ancient Rome but vermouth (from the German word *Wermut*, 'wormwood' one of its early ingredients) as we know it today seems to have evolved in Germany or Italy in the later Middle Ages. There are both sweet (mostly Italian) and dry vermouths and the words 'Italian' and 'French' are sometimes used to mean 'sweet' and 'dry'.

The best known are the Italian brands, such as Martini, Cinzano and Riccadonna, and French brands, such as Noilly Prat, Chambery and Lillet, the Italian types being generally reckoned somewhat heavier. Among the French range Chambery and Lillet are something of a cult. Recipes sometimes specify the vermouth ingredient by brand names but, since vermouth cocktails are among the oldest and have for the most part many variants, such precision mostly reflects the personal taste of the recipe writer. Start with your own preferences among the sweet and dry vermouths and experiment. Bianco and rosé vermouths are now very popular—the recipes on the chart should suggest many ideas for the inventive reader who prefers these types.

VERMOUTH

	Gin	Whisky	Brandy	Rum	Sherry/Port
Sweet	Gin and It Martini Million Dollar Palomino	Manhattan Rob Roy	Brandy Vermouth Carol Harvard Karpathian Blood	Genoese Admiral Little Princess	Adonis
Dry	Bronx Terrace Martini Roselyn Three Stripes	Hole in One Miami Beach Wembley		Beelzebub	Bamboo Reform Devil's Cocktail
Sweet & Dry	Bloodhound Bronx Hotel Plaza Martini Queen's Trinity	Affinity		Mr Giovanni	Bamboo Savoy

ADONIS

1 part sweet vermouth ● 1 part dry sherry ● 1 dash bitters

Stir and add a twist of orange peel.

AFFINITY

1 part whisky ● 1 part sweet vermouth

1 part dry vermouth ● 2 dashes bitters

Stir and add a twist of lemon peel.

BAMBOO REFORM

1 part dry vermouth ● 2 parts dry sherry ● 1 dash orange bitters

Stir and serve with a cherry.

BAMBOO SAVOY

1 part dry vermouth ● 1 part sweet vermouth ● 2 parts dry sherry

Stir.

BEELZEBUB

3 parts rum ● 1 part dry vermouth

Stir and serve with a black olive.

BLOODHOUND

2 parts gin ● 1 part sweet vermouth ● 1 part dry vermouth

Shake then decorate with two or three crushed strawberries. Alternatively, mix all the ingredients in the electric blender with crushed ice.

BRANDY VERMOUTH

4 parts brandy ● 1 part sweet vermouth ● 1 dash bitters per drink

Stir.

BRONX

3 parts gin ● 1 part sweet vermouth

1 part dry vermouth ● 1 part orange juice

Shake. This has two interesting relatives. **Bronx Golden:** add an egg yolk and dash of powdered sugar to the above. Shake. **Bronx Silver:** add the white of an egg and powdered sugar to the Bronx recipe. Shake.

BRONX TERRACE

2 parts gin ● 2 parts dry vermouth ● 1 part fresh lime juice

Shake and decorate with half a cherry.

CAROL

2 parts brandy ● 1 part sweet vermouth

Stir. Add a cherry or, if you prefer, an onion.

DEVIL'S COCKTAIL

1 part port ● 1 part dry vermouth ● 2 dashes lemon juice

Shake.

GENOESE ADMIRAL

3 parts rum ● 1 part sweet vermouth

2 barspoons orange juice ● 1 barspoon lemon juice

Shake.

GIN AND IT

1 or 2 parts gin ● 1 part sweet vermouth

Pour the ingredients in your preferred proportions into a glass without ice and stir.

HARVARD

2 parts brandy ● 1 part sweet vermouth ● 1 barspoon grenadine

2 barspoons lemon juice ● 1 dash bitters

Shake.

HOLE IN ONE

7 parts whisky ● 3 parts dry vermouth

2 dashes lemon juice per drink ● 1 dash orange bitters per drink

Shake.

HOTEL PLAZA

1 part gin ● 1 part sweet vermouth ● 1 part dry vermouth

Shake and serve with a slice of crushed pineapple. For **Queen's Cocktail** add 1 part pineapple juice to the shaker and omit the decorative slice.

KARPATHIAN BLOOD

2 parts brandy ● 1 part sweet vermouth

2 barspoons orange juice ● 1 dash bitters

Shake.

LITTLE PRINCESS

1 part white rum ● 1 part sweet vermouth

Stir.

MANHATTAN

See *Bourbon* page 93

THE MARTINI

A classic with its own section on pages 29–30

MIAMI BEACH

A variant of the **Wembley** below

MILLION DOLLAR COCKTAIL

2 parts gin ● 1 part sweet vermouth

2 barspoons pineapple juice per drink

1 barspoon grenadine per drink ● 1 egg white per 2 drinks

Shake.

MR GIOVANNI

2 parts rum ● 2 parts sweet vermouth

1 part dry vermouth ● 3 barspoons orange juice per drink

1 barspoon lime juice cordial per drink

Shake.

PALOMINO

4 parts gin ● 1 part sweet vermouth ● 1 part grapefruit juice

---

Shake.

QUEEN'S COCKTAIL

A variant of **Hotel Plaza**, opposite

ROB ROY

2 parts whisky ● 1 part sweet vermouth ● 2 dashes bitters

Stir.

ROSELYN

2 parts gin ● 1 part dry vermouth ● 1 barspoon grenadine

Shake and add a twist of lemon peel.

THREE STRIPES

2 parts gin ● 1 part dry vermouth ● 1 part orange juice

Shake. One recipe substitutes actual slices of orange for the orange juice in the shaker.

TRINITY

1 part gin ● 1 part sweet vermouth ● 1 part dry vermouth

Stir. This is sometimes given as the recipe for the **Perfect Martini**. A stronger (more perfect?) recipe will be found in the **Martini** section.

WEMBLEY

1 part whisky ● 1 part dry vermouth ● 1 part pineapple juice

Shake. The **Miami Beach** has grapefruit in place of the pineapple juice. Try serving either recipe on the rocks with a cherry on a stick.

The Martini

A **Martinez** cocktail devised in the 1860s (and sometimes called the **Matinez**) comprised gin, vermouth and maraschino. Today, the name is given to drinks comprising only gin and vermouth. The main classifications are **Sweet**, made with sweet vermouth, the **Medium**, made with sweet and dry, and the **Dry** made with dry. Proportions vary in every department though every authority claims theirs as the definitive one. Here are a few to start you off in quest of your own 'definitive' version.

THE SWEET MARTINI

1 part gin ● 1 part sweet vermouth

or alternatively:

2 parts gin ● 1 part sweet vermouth

1 dash orange bitters (optional)

Serve with a cherry or even, it has been suggested, an olive.

THE MEDIUM MARTINI

2 or 3 parts gin ● 1 part sweet vermouth ● 1 part dry vermouth

or:

1 part gin ● 1 part sweet vermouth ● 1 part dry vermouth
This one is also called **Trinity** and even the **Perfect Martini**!

Yet another recipe suggests:

4 parts gin ● 1 part sweet vermouth ● 1 part dry vermouth
Also called the **Perfect Martini** with rather better justification.

Since all ingredients are clear, all these drinks should be stirred. Most people like a twist of lemon peel with the medium martinis.

The Dry Martini

About 1910, it is supposed, a Signor Martini, head barman at New York's Knickerbocker Hotel, transformed the then popular **Gin and French** by stirring equal quantities of gin and Noilly Prat dry vermouth, with a dash of orange bitters, pouring the mix into a cocktail glass, twisting a zest of lemon peel over it and serving it up with a green olive on a stick. Like any good myth, this gives a convincing explanation of a mystery—and the mystique surrounding the **Dry Martini** makes the lore of the French wine connoisseur seem like kindergarten stuff.

The orange bitters (not a very good idea) were soon forgotten but the primitive 1:1 ratio survived in some quarters into the 1950s. In more advanced circles it had already shifted to 2 gin: 1 vermouth before the First World War and the trend thus established was to culminate in our own time in the **Naked Martini**—straight gin, stirred on ice and served with an olive. Somewhere in between you will find your preference. Mine is: 7 parts gin, 1 part dry vermouth. For some this is an **Extra Dry** for others it is strictly for the kids—they prefer, let us say, 12 or 15 parts of gin to 1 of vermouth. Whatever you consider the correct version of the **Dry Martini**, serve it as cold as possible and use the best ingredients you can—the finest London Dry Gin and the best Italian or French dry vermouth. And I like that olive and twist of lemon peel. The **Gibson** is a **Dry Martini** served with an onion; the **Boston Bullet** a **Dry Martini** served with an olive stuffed with an almond; the **Vodkatini** and **Tequini**, quaint variants of this classic made with vodka or tequila.

The Classics

At this point we leave the charts for a while for a look at some of the classic styles and cocktails, some more than a century old, others made fashionable in the Twenties or later. In alphabetical order, some of the best-known classic styles are: the **Cobbler**, a drink of wine or spirit flavoured with sugar syrup or a fruit liqueur; the **Collins**, known both as the **Tom Collins** (originally made with Old Tom sweetened gin) and the **John Collins**, and basically a bar-made lemonade spiked with gin; the **Highball**, origin obscure and best defined as a spirit-based, iced drink mixed with any carbonated beverage; the **Mint Julep**, the drink of the American South which you will find among the Bourbon recipes on page 93; the **Rickey**, a variant of the **Collins**; the **Sangaree**; the **Sling**, perhaps the oldest of all mixed drinks; and, finally, the **Sour**, the combination of a spirit, citrus fruit and sweetener which has given rise to many of the basic cocktail recipes.

ALEXANDER

1 part brandy ● 1 part crème de cacao ● 1 part cream

Shake. Dust with a little nutmeg and serve. This is sometimes called the **Brandy Alexander**. For the **Gin Alexander** or **Princess Mary**, replace the brandy with gin. You will find Tia Maria makes an acceptable substitution for the crème de cacao, whatever your purists friends may say.

BLOODY MARY

1 part vodka ● 4 parts tomato juice

2 dashes Worcestershire sauce per drink

1 barspoon lemon juice per drink

1 barspoon tomato ketchup per drink

Celery salt, tabasco sauce and pepper to taste

The tomato ketchup is suggested by Kingsley Amis in his book *On Drink* and is well worth trying. Emulsify the ketchup, vodka, Worcestershire sauce and celery salt in a mixing bowl. Pour the tomato juice and lemon into the mixing jug and stir in the vodka mixture. Add ice and stir again. Decorate, if you wish, with a slice of lemon adding tabasco sauce and pepper to taste.

BOSOM CARESSER

2 parts brandy ● 1 part curacao (orange or white)

1 barspoon grenadine per drink ● 1 egg yolk per two drinks

Shake. Another recipe with this name calls for 2 parts brandy; 2 parts madeira wine; 1 part curacao.

CARUSO

1 part gin ● 1 part dry vermouth ● 1 part green crème de menthe.

Stir. Sometimes the proportions are given as: 3 parts gin; 1 part dry vermouth; 1 part crème de menthe.

CLARIDGE

2 parts gin ● 2 parts dry vermouth

1 part Cointreau ● 1 part apricot brandy

Stir.

CLOVER CLUB

6 parts gin ● 2 parts lemon juice

1 part grenadine ● 1 egg white per two drinks

Shake well and serve in a wine glass.

John Collins (left); Bloody Mary (mint optional).

Left to right: Crème de Menthe; Flying Boat (front); Hotel Plaza (back);
Horse's Neck Highball.

COBBLER

Any wine, spirit, port or sherry

1 barspoon curacao and/or sugar syrup

Fill a wine goblet with ice. Fill a little more than half with the preferred wine or spirit. Add the curacao and/or sugar syrup. Stir. Decorate with fruit slices and/or a sprig of mint and serve with straws.

COLLINS

1 good measure of gin ● juice of 1 lemon

1 barspoon sugar syrup ● soda water

Use a tall, straight-sided tumbler of at least 6 ounces capacity. Mix the lemon juice and sugar syrup in the glass, or in a jug if a number of drinks are being made. Pour into the glass, add ice and top up with soda water. Stir gently. Decorate with fruit slices and a sprig of mint and serve with straws. You can substitute other spirits for the gin to produce the **Whisky**, **Colonel** (i.e. Bourbon), **Rum** or **Brandy Collins**.

CORPSE REVIVER

2 parts brandy ● 1 part sweet vermouth ● 1 part Calvados

Stir. You may prefer equal proportions, especially if you are using a fine Calvados.

DAIQUIRI

4 parts white rum ● 1 part lime juice

1 dash sugar syrup per drink

Shake. You may prefer to use powdered sugar or, alternatively, replace the sugar altogether with a dash of grenadine for a **Pink Daiquiri** or **Bacardi**.

EGG NOG

A drink combining alcohol with egg and milk or cream, and decorated with grated nutmeg. **Nogs** may be mixed in quantity or individually.

STANDARD NOG

1 part rum, port or sherry • 1 barspoon brandy or liqueur

1 barspoon sugar syrup • 1 whole egg • 3 parts milk or single cream

Shake, strain into a goblet or tumbler and sprinkle with grated nutmeg.

BREAKFAST EGG NOG

1 part brandy • 1 part Cointreau

1 dash chocolate or coffee liqueur • 3 parts milk or single cream

1 whole egg per drink

Shake and serve as above.

GIMLET

1 or 2 parts gin • 1 part lime juice cordial

Stir. As Philip Marlowe learnt in *The Long Goodbye* the 'correct' recipe is equal parts of gin and Rose's lime juice but, according to some, one may even add soda.

GODFATHER

2 parts whisky • 1 part Amaretto di Saronno

Pour the whisky over ice in a small tumbler and float the Amaretto on top. For a **Godmother** substitute vodka for the whisky. Some prefer to stir the ingredients on the ice.

HARVEY WALLBANGER

2 parts vodka • 1 part Galliano • 6 parts orange juice

Pour the vodka and orange juice over ice in a tall glass and float the Galliano on top. You can, of course, increase the proportion of vodka.

HIGHBALL

1 good measure of any spirit from apple brandy to whisky

1 dash of bitters or grenadine, optional

soda water, ginger ale or any other mixer of your choice

Stir. Traditionalists may say that the classic **Highball** should not include fruit juices as mixers but more than 30 recipes in one American cocktail book disregard this rule.

HORSE'S NECK HIGHBALL

1 measure brandy or rye whiskey ● ginger ale

Carefully peel the rind from a lemon spiral fashion; place it in a tall glass with one end hanging over the rim. Fill the glass with ice cubes, pour over the spirit and a dash of bitters if desired and stir.

MARGARITA

4 parts tequila ● 1 part curacao ● 1 part lemon or lime juice

Shake and strain into a chilled glass which has been rimmed in lemon juice and salt.

OLD FASHIONED

See Bourbon page 94

PINA COLADA

3 parts white rum ● 4 parts pineapple juice ● 2 parts coconut cream

Blend with crushed ice and pour into a large goblet or a hollowed-out pineapple half. Decorate with a slice of pineapple and a cherry. Serve with straws.

PRAIRIE OYSTER

3 barspoons Worcestershire sauce ● 1 barspoon tomato ketchup

1 barspoon vinegar ● 1 egg yolk ● pepper (preferably cayenne)

Stir the first three ingredients in a small wine glass, add the egg yolk without breaking it, sprinkle some pepper on top and swallow. This is the classic pick-me-up but some recommend adding an ounce or so of brandy (see *Basic Cupboard* page 19). Shake it together with the first three ingredients, pour into the glass and proceed as above. Others swear by alcoholic bitters such as Fernet Branca or Underbug. The aim, of course, is to cure the hangover—may the magic work!

PUNCH

Not strictly speaking a cocktail but here is a basic recipe for a pleasant winter party drink.

SOUTH GATE MANOR PUNCH (50 glasses approx)

6 bottles red Bordeaux wine ● 1 bottle Tarragona or port

1 tumbler brandy ● 1 small wine glass orange liqueur ● 3 oranges

2 lemons ● cloves ● sticks of cinnamon ● 2 pints water

Stick one orange with cloves and roast it in the oven—this is worth the trouble. Slice the remaining fruit and put it with water in a large preserving pan. Bring near the boil and stir in the other ingredients. Return the pan close to the boil and serve the punch in a large bowl with the stuck orange floating on top. Serve hot and keep hot, but never boil punch as this drives off the alcohol.

RICKEY

This is really a **Collins** in which fresh lime juice substitutes for the lemon juice. The **Gin Rickey** and the **Sloe Gin Rickey** are well known, but a delicious variant is made with Mandarine Napoleon and other liqueurs can be used—apricot brandy for the **Apricot Rickey** and so on.

SANGAREE

A wine or spirit is sweetened to taste with sugar syrup, served on ice with a dusting of nutmeg on top. In the case of a spirit base the liquor is generally cut half and half with water.

SCREWDRIVER

The earliest **Screwdriver** was no doubt a variant of the **Orange Blossom**: 2 parts gin: 1 part orange juice; dash of powdered sugar; shake. You substitute vodka and may omit the sugar syrup, or change the proportions to 1 part vodka and 2–4 parts orange juice and merely pour the ingredients into the glass. In all cases, serve on ice and decorate with a slice of orange.

SIDECAR

2 parts brandy ● 1 part curacao or Cointreau ● 1 part lemon juice

Shake.

SLING

One of the oldest of mixed drinks and no doubt the ancestor of the **Collins**, the **Sling** combines a spirit with sugar and lemon juice, but includes other ingredients. A renowned version is the **Singapore Sling**.

3 parts gin ● 1 part cherry brandy ● juice of 1 lemon

Shake and strain into a tall, ice-filled glass, top up with soda water and decorate with slices of orange, lemon or lime and a cherry. Some versions have lime in place of the lemon juice and others add one part of Benedictine.

SOUR

3 parts spirit ● 1 part lime juice ● 1 barspoon sugar syrup

Proportions are a subject of debate, even controversy—a rule of thumb used to be '1 sweet, 2 sour, 3 strong'. Lemon juice can replace the lime. Shake, or stir vigorously in a jug for large quantities. Decorate with half a slice of lemon and add a cherry. The classics are the **Scotch Sour** and the **Whiskey Sour**, made with rye whiskey.

SPRITZER HIGHBALL

1 part white wine ● 1 part soda water

Pour in equal measures over ice in wine goblet. The name derives from the German word *spritzig*, 'fizzy, lively', and the wine was originally made with Rhine wine—the poet Byron's Hock and Soda Water.

SUNRISE

2 parts tequila ● 1 part crème de banane ● 1 part Galliano

1 part cream ● 1 dash grenadine per drink ● 1 dash lemon juice per drink

Shake. Pour into a wine goblet, decorate with a wheel of orange on the edge of the glass and serve with straws.

WHITE LADY

2 parts gin ● 1 part Cointreau

1 part lemon juice ● 1 egg white per four drinks

Shake.

Orange Style

Curacao (or curaçao, pronounced kura-soh) was the first of the orange liqueurs. Originally, it appears, they were rum-based cordials made by the planters of the Dutch West Indies and flavoured with the rind of the bitter oranges of the island of Curacao. Today the liqueurs are distilled from grape spirit infused with orange peel. Curacaos come in green, white, blue and orange colourings. Grand Marnier is a French variant of curacao invented in the 1860s, with a brandy base which can be detected as an aftertaste, and having the colour of pale brandy. Cointreau, another French variant manufactured in Angers, is also brandy based, but has a somewhat fuller flavour and is colourless. Curacao as such is somewhat sweeter than either and Triple Sec, despite its name, probably the sweetest drink known. I recommend a good curacao for all the recipes in this section, though some (as indicated in parentheses) specify Cointreau.

Mandarine Napoleon, a Belgian liqueur flavoured with tangerine peel, is extremely sweet and characteristic in flavour. Van der Hum (Africaans for 'Mr. What's his name') is a South African liqueur on the tangerine theme.

The chart in this section is the first of six for various liqueur flavours. At the top you will see the name of the relevant liqueur (orange in this case) indicating that all the recipes in the chart will be for the liqueur of that type. The final column contains recipes which require only the liqueur and one of the spirits with the addition of juices or other non-alcoholic ingredients. In a few instances you will find the recipe calls only for the alcoholic ingredients.

ORANGE

	Dry Vermouth	Sweet Vermouth	Sherry/Port	Aperitif	Extras
Gin	Snake in the Grass	The Baron Damn the Weather Guards	Bartender		Maiden's Prayer White Lady
Whisky	Regimental Beauty	Churchill	Sherry Twist		Silent Third
Vodka	Flying Boat			Jeffrey's Question	Balalaika
Rum	Silver Memories	Fair and Warm	Beachcomber's Find		Mandarin Dynasty Parisian Blonde
Brandy	Green Room		Betsy Ross	Dutch Uncle	Between the Sheets Sidecar

BALALAIKA

2 parts vodka ● 1 part curacao (Cointreau) ● 1 part lemon juice

Shake.

THE BARON

3 parts gin ● 1 part dry vermouth

½ barspoon sweet vermouth per drink ● 1½ barspoons curacao per drink

Stir and add a twist of lemon peel.

BARTENDER

1 part gin ● 2 dashes bitters

1 barspoon curacao (Grand Marnier) per drink

1 part dry sherry ● 1 part Dubonnet

Stir. Another recipe suggests that you substitute 1 part dry vermouth for the bitters.

BEACHCOMBER'S FIND

3 parts rum ● 1 dash port per drink

1 part curacao ● 1 part lime juice

Shake and pour into a cocktail glass with its rim moistened and crusted with castor sugar. Decorate with a maraschino cherry.

BETSY ROSS

1 part brandy ● 1 part port ● 1 dash curacao per drink

Stir. Add a twist of lemon peel.

BETWEEN THE SHEETS

2 parts brandy ● 2 parts golden or white rum

1 part curacao (or Cointreau) ● 1 barspoon lemon juice per drink

Shake and add a twist of lemon. An earlier version reads: 3 parts brandy; 3 parts rum; 1 part Cointreau; 2 barspoons lime juice.

CHURCHILL

3 parts whisky ● 1 part sweet vermouth

2 barspoons curacao per drink ● 2 barspoons lime juice per drink

Shake.

DAMN THE WEATHER

2 parts gin • 1 part sweet vermouth

1 barspoon curacao per drink • 1 part orange juice

Shake.

DUTCH UNCLE

1 part brandy • 1 part curacao

1 part Dubonnet • 1 part lemon juice

Shake.

FAIR AND WARM

3 parts rum • 1 part sweet vermouth • 2 barspoons curacao per drink

Shake.

FLYING BOAT

3 parts vodka • 1 part dry vermouth • 1 part blue curacao

Shake and pour into a tumbler with ice cubes.

GREEN ROOM

2 parts brandy • 1 part dry vermouth

1 barspoon curacao (Grand Marnier)

Stir.

GUARDS

2 parts gin • 1 part sweet vermouth • 1 barspoon Cointreau

Stir.

JEFFREY'S QUESTION

1 part vodka ● 2 barspoons curacao per drink

1 part Dubonnet ● 1 dash Angostura bitters per drink

1 egg white per 4 drinks

Shake.

MAIDEN'S PRAYER

3 parts gin ● 2 parts curacao (Cointreau) ● 1 part lemon juice

---

Shake.

MANDARIN DYNASTY

3 parts white rum ● 2 parts Mandarine Napoleon

1 part lemon juice ● 1 barspoon grenadine

Shake.

PARISIAN BLONDE

1 part rum ● 1 part curacao ● 1 part cream

Shake.

REGIMENTAL BEAUTY

2 parts whisky ● 1 part dry vermouth ● 1 barspoon curacao

Stir.

SHERRY TWIST

1 part whisky ● 2 parts sherry

1 part curacao ● 2 dashes lemon juice per drink

Shake and serve with a twist of orange peel and sprinkling of cinnamon.

SIDECAR

See *Classics* page 37

SILENT THIRD

1 part whisky ● 1 part curacao (Cointreau) ● 1 part lemon juice

Shake.

SILVER MEMORIES

3 parts white rum ● 1 part dry vermouth ● 1 part curacao

Stir.

SNAKE IN THE GRASS

2 parts gin ● 1 part dry vermouth

1 part curacao (Cointreau) ● 1 part lemon juice

Shake. The snake here is undoubtedly the dry vermouth; its fangs are more apparent if you mix equal proportions of the ingredients.

WHITE LADY

See *Classics* page 38

Anis & Others

Pernod is the best known drink in this group. It descends from the original Absinthe, invented in the mid-eighteenth century as a medicinal preparation of alcohol, aniseed, liquorice, wormwood and various herbs by a French doctor. In the 1790s he sold the recipe to the Parisian firm of *Pernod fils*, who continued to market the drink until the year 1915. But the bitter-tasting drink had by that time earned an evil reputation, being held to drive its addicts mad. All its bad effects were attributed, not to its high alcohol content, but to the wormwood which gave it its characteristic flavour. Accordingly, in 1915, the French government banned the use of this extract and since that time true Absinthe has been impossible to obtain legally. Nevertheless, because it is a convenient general term for the various liquorice and/or aniseed-flavoured drinks related to it, the word is still often used in cocktail recipes. In using the recipes in this book select the one you prefer or the one you have to hand but remember that the flavour of Pernod is extremely pervasive.

Anisette, first marketed by Marie Brizard at Bordeaux in the mid-eighteenth century, is a sweet, anis-flavoured liqueur less powerful than Pernod in its effect; and pastis, manufactured in Marseilles, is a liquorice-based liqueur also less strongly flavoured than Pernod.

ABSINTHE

	Sweet Vermouth	Dry Vermouth	Aperitif	Extras
Gin	Jeyplak	Deep Sea Piccadilly Peggy		Café de Paris Monkey Gland Wax
Whisky		Whizz Bang		Linstead
Vodka	Fifth Degree Macaroni	Vodka Du Barry	Transparent	
Rum			Country Girls	Shanghai
Brandy	Presto		Phoebe Snow	Absolute

ABSOLUTE

2 parts brandy ● 1 part absinthe

Stir.

CAFE DE PARIS

1 measure gin ● 3 dashes anisette per drink

1 barspoon cream per drink ● 1 egg white

Shake.

COUNTRY GIRLS

2 parts white rum ● 1 part Pernod

2 parts Campari ● 2 dashes grenadine

Stir. Decorate with a cherry and a slice of orange.

DEEP SEA COCKTAIL

1 part gin ● 1 part dry vermouth

1 dash absinthe per drink ● 1 dash orange bitters per drink

Stir. Add a twist of lemon peel and a green olive.

FIFTH DEGREE

1 part vodka ● 1 part dry vermouth

1 part sweet vermouth ● 1 barspoon absinthe

Stir. Another vermouth-absinthe recipe, the **Macaroni**, calls for: 1 part sweet vermouth; 2 parts absinthe; 1 part vodka. Stir.

JEYPLAK

2 parts gin ● 1 part sweet vermouth ● 1 dash absinthe

Stir. Add a twist of lemon peel and serve with a cherry.

LINSTEAD

1 part whisky ● 1 part sweetened pineapple juice

1 dash absinthe ● 1 dash powdered sugar

Shake. This Scotch version of an American recipe is, to my taste, better with rye whiskey. If you do use rye, add a dash of lemon juice.

MACARONI

See **Fifth Degree**, above.

MONKEY GLAND

3 parts gin ● 2 dashes absinthe

2 parts orange juice ● 2 dashes grenadine

Shake.

PEGGY COCKTAIL

2 parts gin ● 1 part dry vermouth

1 dash absinthe ● 2 dashes Dubonnet

Shake.

PHOEBE SNOW

1 part brandy ● 1 dash absinthe

1 part Dubonnet

Shake.

PICCADILLY

2 parts gin ● 1 part dry vermouth

1 dash absinthe ● 1 dash grenadine

Shake.

PRESTO

3 parts brandy ● 1 part sweet vermouth

1 dash absinthe per drink ● 1 part orange juice

Shake.

SHANGHAI

4 parts dark rum ● 1 part anisette

3 parts lemon juice ● 2 dashes grenadine per drink

Shake.

Left to right: Singapore Slings; Gibson; Clover Club; Bloodhound.

Pippin Cold Punch (made with tea).

TRANSPARENT

1 part vodka ● 1 part Dubonnet ● 1 dash absinthe

Stir.

VODKA DU BARRY

2 parts vodka ● 1 part dry vermouth

1 barspoon absinthe ● 1 dash bitters

Stir and add a slice of orange.

WAX

1 part gin ● 1 part absinthe ● 3 dashes sugar syrup

1 dash bitters ● 1 egg white

Shake.

WHIZZ BANG

2 parts whisky ● 1 part dry vermouth ● 2 dashes absinthe

2 dashes grenadine ● 2 dashes bitters

Shake.

The Apricot Effect

The term apricot brandy is now generally used to mean apricot-flavoured liqueurs. In my opinion, the best of these is the Bols, being somewhat drier than most other brands, such as De Kuyper. However, they all tend to be somewhat sweet and you may wish to adjust the quantities in the recipes in this section for a drier result.

There are true apricot brandies, but they are generally expensive and difficult to obtain.

APRICOT

	Dry Vermouth	Sweet Vermouth	Sherry/Port	Aperitif	Extras
Gin	Favourite				Bermudan Rose Fairy Belle Paradise Rosy Skies
Whisky		Never Never		Scotch Dandy	King George VI
Vodka	Tsarina		Little Natasha	Shimmering Summer	Amity
Rum	Cynic	Apple Pie			Hop Toad
Brandy	Hussar	Black Tulip	Strong Temptation		Cubano

AMITY

3 parts vodka ● 1 part apricot brandy ● 4 parts lemon juice

3 dashes bitters per drink ● 2 dashes grenadine per

drink ● pineapple juice

Shake all the ingredients except the pineapple juice. Strain into an ice-filled tall glass and top up with the pineapple juice. Stir.

APPLE PIE

1 part white rum ● 1 part sweet vermouth

1 barspoon apricot brandy

1 barspoon lemon juice ● 2 dashes grenadine

Shake.

BERMUDAN ROSE

3 parts gin ● 1 part apricot brandy ● 1 barspoon grenadine per drink

1 barspoon lemon juice per drink

Shake.

BLACK TULIP

3 parts brandy ● 1 part sweet vermouth

1 barspoon apricot brandy per drink ● 1 dash bitters per drink

Stir and serve with a black olive.

CUBANO

2 parts brandy ● 1 part apricot brandy

1 barspoon lime juice cordial

Stir and add a slice of orange.

CYNIC

2 parts white rum ● 1 part dry vermouth ● 1 part apricot brandy
1 part lemon juice ● 1 barspoon powdered sugar per 2 drinks

Shake.

FAIRY BELLE

3 parts gin ● 1 part apricot brandy ● 1 egg white per drink
1 barspoon grenadine per drink

Shake.

FAVOURITE

1 part gin ● 1 part dry vermouth
1 part apricot brandy ● 1 dash lemon juice

Shake. There is a cluster of recipes using these ingredients in varying
proportions of which this, as the name suggests, is probably the best.
Try doubling the proportion of gin and adding a dash of grenadine.

HOP TOAD

2 parts rum ● 1 part apricot brandy
2 barspoons lemon juice ● 1 dash bitters

Shake. There is also a rumless **Hop Toad**, sometimes called the **Bullfrog**.

HUSSAR

3 parts brandy ● 1 part dry vermouth
1 barspoon apricot brandy per drink ● 1 dash bitters per drink

Stir.

KING GEORGE VI

2 parts whisky ● 1 part apricot brandy
2 parts orange juice ● 1 part lemon juice

Shake and serve in a wine glass.

LITTLE NATASHA

1 part vodka ● 1 part apricot brandy ● 1 barspoon port

1 egg per 2 drinks ● powdered sugar to taste

Shake, strain into a wine glass and dust with cinnamon.

NEVER NEVER

2 parts whisky ● 1 part sweet vermouth

2 dashes apricot brandy

Stir.

PARADISE

1 part gin ● 1 part apricot brandy ● 1 part orange juice

Shake.

ROSY SKIES

3 parts gin ● 1 part apricot brandy

1 part lemon juice ● 2 dashes grenadine per drink

Shake. Also known as **Good Night Ladies**.

SCOTCH DANDY

2 parts whisky ● 2 dashes apricot brandy per drink

1 part Dubonnet ● 1 part orange juice

1 dash sugar syrup per drink

Shake and add a cherry.

SHIMMERING SUMMER

3 parts vodka ● 1 part apricot brandy ● 1 barspoon Campari per drink

1 part lemon juice ● 1 egg white per four drinks ● orange juice

Shake all ingredients except the orange juice. Strain into an ice-filled tall glass and top up with orange juice. Decorate with an orange slice and cherry and serve with straws.

STRONG TEMPTATION

1 barspoon brandy ● 1 part apricot brandy ● 1 part port

Stir.

TSARINA

2 parts vodka ● 1 part dry vermouth

1 part apricot brandy ● 1 dash lime juice cordial per drink

Stir.

The Coffee Complex

This chart represents a combination of recipes based on coffee and chocolate-flavoured liqueurs. The best known are the chocolate crème de cacao, white or brown; the coffee Tia Maria, a rum-based liqueur from Jamaica; and Kahlua, from Mexico.

I have specified the liqueur called for in the traditional versions of these recipes but it is obvious, despite what the purists may say, that you can substitute any of them for each other. The alternatives may be different, they are also delicious. Tia Maria is probably the most popular of the coffee liqueurs, though some people prefer the somewhat lighter flavour of Kahlua.

COFFEE/CACAO

	Dry Vermouth	Sherry/Port	Aperitif	Extras
Gin	Maxim			Gin Alexander Princess Maria Suwannee Russian Cocktail
Vodka	Rapid Fire	Princess Belle		Black Russian Ninotchka
Rum	Topical	Aunty's Breakfast	Jamaican Dude	Artemesia Tropic Cream
Brandy	Chocolate Soldier Dark Coffee	Jamaican Hope		Brandy Alexander

ARTEMESIA

3 parts rum ● 1 part Kahlua ● 1 egg white per two drinks

Shake. Dust with nutmeg.

AUNTY'S BREAKFAST

3 parts white rum ● 2 parts Tia Maria ● 1 part sherry

2 barspoons lime or lemon juice per drink ● 1 egg white per 2 drinks

Shake.

BLACK RUSSIAN

2 parts vodka ● 1 part coffee liqueur

Pour over ice cubes in the order given. For a **White Russian** float a measure of cream on top.

BRANDY ALEXANDER

See *Classics* page 31

CHOCOLATE SOLDIER

1 part brandy ● 1 part dry vermouth

1 part crème de cacao ● 2 dashes orange bitters

Shake.

DARK COFFEE

1 part brandy ● 1 part dry vermouth

1 part Tia Maria ● 2 dashes Angostura bitters

Shake.

GIN ALEXANDER

1 part gin ● 1 part crème de cacao (brown) ● 1 part cream

Shake. For **Princess Maria**, substitute Tia Maria for the crème de cacao.

JAMAICAN DUDE

2 parts white rum ● 2 parts Tia Maria

1 part Dubonnet per drink ● 1 egg yolk per drink

Shake.

JAMAICAN HOPE

1 part brandy ● 1 dash port ● 1 part crème de cacao

Stir.

MAXIM

3 parts gin ● 2 parts dry vermouth

1 dash crème de cacao per drink

Stir.

NINOTCHKA

3 parts vodka ● 1 part crème de cacao

2 barspoons lemon juice per drink

Shake.

PRINCESS BELLE

3 parts vodka ● 2 parts Tia Maria

1 part sherry ● 2 barspoons lime juice per drink

Shake.

PRINCESS MARIA

See **Gin Alexander**, above.

RAPID FIRE

3 parts vodka ● 2 barspoons dry vermouth per drink

2 parts Tia Maria

Shake.

RUSSIAN COCKTAIL

1 part vodka ● 1 part gin ● 1 part crème de cacao

Shake.

SUWANNEE

1 part gin ● 2 dashes crème de cacoa per drink

1 part fresh orange juice ● 1 egg white per 2 drinks

Shake.

TOPICAL

1 part white rum ● 1 part dry vermouth ● 2 parts Kahlua

1 barspoon grenadine per drink ● 1 dash bitters per drink

Shake.

TROPIC CREAM

3 parts white rum ● 1 part Kahlua

2 barspoons cream per drink

Shake.

Crème de la Crème

During the 1930s crème de banane was one of the most fashionable liqueurs with cocktail enthusiasts, while crème de menthe is still one of the most popular, especially as an after dinner digestive. **Crème de Menthe Frappé** is probably the best-known method of serving this liqueur. Fill a medium, stemmed wine glass, or a champagne flute with crushed ice and pour the liqueur over it. You can, of course, serve any liqueur in this way. Crème de Menthe comes as both a white and a green liqueur.

Since the 1940s **Kir**, white wine flavoured with crème de cassis, has established itself as something of a classic, having been first popularized in Dijon where crème de cassis is manufactured from blackcurrant.

CREME DE BANANE

BALROG

1 dash white rum ● 1 part crème de cacao

1 part crème de banane ● 2 parts cream

Shake. Pour over ice cubes in a wine goblet. You can add a dash of grenadine if desired.

BARBADIAN TSAR

3 parts vodka ● 1 part crème de banane ● orange juice

Stir vodka and crème de banane. Pour over ice cubes in a tall glass, fill with orange juice and stir.

GUADELOUPE

1 part white rum ● 1 part crème de banane

1 part orange juice ● 1 egg white per 2 drinks

Shake. Decorate with a slice of pineapple and a cherry.

LAPUTA

3 parts brandy ● 1 part crème de banane

1 barspoon orange juice per drink ● 2 barspoons lemon juice per drink

Shake.

SILVER JUBILEE

2 parts gin ● 1 part crème de banane ● 1 part cream

Shake.

CREME DE CASSIS

KIR

Put two good barspoons of crème de cassis in a wine glass and top up with chilled white wine.

PARISIAN

1 part gin ● 1 part dry vermouth ● 1 part crème de cassis

Stir. Some recipes call for two parts gin.

CRÈME DE MENTHE

ALEXANDER'S SISTER

1 part gin ● 1 part crème de menthe ● 1 part cream

Shake.

AMERICAN BEAUTY

1 part brandy ● 1 part dry vermouth

1 dash crème de menthe (white) per drink ● 1 barspoon port

1 part grenadine ● 1 part orange juice

Shake and strain into a wine glass and float port on the top. You may like to try this with more brandy—one recipe recommends 4 parts.

COLD DECK

2 parts brandy ● 1 part sweet vermouth

1 part crème de menthe (white)

Stir.

FALLEN ANGEL

3 parts gin ● 2 dashes crème de menthe per drink

1 part lemon juice ● 1 dash Angostura bitters per drink

Shake. Again, white is preferable but the colour is all right even if green is used. For a change, substitute fresh lime for the lemon juice and serve with a cherry.

GRASSHOPPER

1 part crème de cacao ● 1 part crème de menthe (white)

1 part cream

Shake.

PALL MALL

1 part gin ● 1 part sweet vermouth ● 1 part dry vermouth

1 barspoon crème de menthe (white) ● 1 or 2 dashes orange juice

Stir or shake. One recipe omits the orange juice and calls for three parts gin to the above proportions of the other ingredients. Stir.

STARBOARD LIGHT

2 parts gin ● 1 part crème de menthe (green)

1 part lemon juice

Shake.

STINGER

2 parts brandy ● 1 part crème de menthe (white)

Stir. The proportions given vary from 1 to 3 parts of brandy.

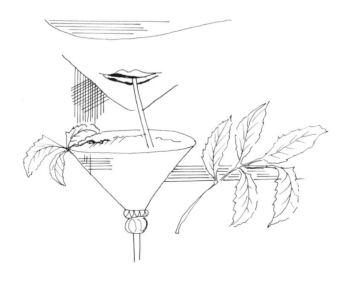

Cherry Delights

A favourite Christmas drink, cherry brandy liqueur is marketed by many famous manufacturers such as Bols, De Kuyper and Peter Heering. You will no doubt have your own favourite which will go nicely in all the recipes on the chart. Being liqueurs, these are all sweet, rather heavy drinks and, despite their names, not true brandies. A liqueur is produced from a base spirit to which is added a flavouring agent—in this case the liquor derived from mascerating cherries and cherry stones. A true fruit brandy is produced by a distillation direct from the fruit itself; in the cherry class the best-known examples are Kirsch and Kirschwasser. They are drier in flavour than the cherry brandy liqueurs and as strong as cognac.

Among the other cherry drinks is the white Italian liqueur, maraschino. Its distinctive almond and slightly bitter taste comes from the fruit and stones of the marasca cherries which provide the flavouring agent for its spirit base. The preserving liquor in a jar of maraschino cocktail cherries has a similar flavour which is so different from the cherry brandies that the **Merry Widow Cocktail (No. 2)** calls for equal parts of maraschino and cherry brandy.

CHERRY

	Dry Vermouth	Sweet Vermouth	Sherry/Port	Extras
Gin	French Rose Gilroy Manoeuvres	Wedding Belles		Heaven Sent Orange Oasis Singapore Sling
Whisky	Whispering Gal Blood and Sand Sandy Lane			
Vodka	Vodka Gilroy	Happy Returns	The Goat	Pontormo Royal Flush Imperial
Brandy		Gdansk Cherry	Captain's Bridge	Brandy Fix Vanderbilt
Rum	Sunshine Number 5		O Porto!	Cherry Rum

BLOOD AND SAND

1 part whisky ● 1 part sweet vermouth

1 part cherry brandy ● 2 barspoons orange juice

Shake.

BRANDY FIX

3 parts brandy ● 1 part cherry brandy

8 parts lemon juice per drink ● 1 barspoon sugar syrup per drink

Pour the ingredients into a large tumbler filled with crushed ice and stir. Serve with straws and decorate with slices of lemon and orange and a cocktail cherry.

Left to right: White Russians; Guadeloupe; Shady.Grove.

CAPTAIN'S BRIDGE

2 parts brandy ● 1 part port ● 2 parts cherry brandy

Stir.

CHERRY RUM

4 parts rum ● 2 barspoons cherry brandy per drink

1 part cream

Shake.

FRENCH ROSE

3 parts gin ● 1 part dry vermouth ● 1 part cherry brandy

Stir.

GDANSK CHERRY

3 parts brandy ● 1 part sweet vermouth

1 barspoon cherry brandy ● 1 dash lemon juice per drink

Shake.

GILROY

1 part gin ● 3 barspoons dry vermouth

1 part cherry brandy ● juice of $\frac{1}{4}$ lemon

1 dash orange bitters

Shake.

THE GOAT

3 parts vodka ● 1 dash port per drink

1 part cherry brandy ● 2 dashes grenadine per drink

Shake.

HAPPY RETURNS

3 parts vodka ● 1 part sweet vermouth ● 1 part cherry brandy

1 part orange juice ● 1 dash lemon juice per drink

Shake. Pour into cocktail glasses and decorate with a cherry.

HEAVEN SENT

1 part gin ● 1 part cherry brandy ● bitter lemon

Pour the gin and cherry brandy over ice in a tumbler. Top up with the bitter lemon and decorate with a slice of lemon.

MANOEUVRES

1 part gin ● 1 part dry vermouth ● 1 part cherry brandy

Stir.

O PORTO!

2 parts rum ● 1 part port ● 1 part cherry brandy

1 white of egg per drink ● $\frac{1}{2}$ barspoon powdered sugar per drink

(optional)

Shake. Serve in a wine glass.

ORANGE OASIS

3 parts gin ● 1 part cherry brandy

8 parts orange juice per drink ● American ginger ale

Shake the gin, cherry brandy and orange juice, pour over ice cubes in a tall glass and top up with ginger ale.

PONTORMO

2 parts vodka ● 1 part cherry brandy ● juice of 1 lime

Shake. Rub the rim of the glass with lime and dip in castor sugar. Fill it with ice cubes, pour in the mixed ingredients and decorate with a wedge of lime and a cherry.

ROYAL FLUSH IMPERIAL

1 part vodka ● 2 parts cherry brandy ● dry ginger ale

Pour the cherry brandy and vodka over ice in a tall glass and top up with the dry ginger ale.

SANDY LANE

3 parts whisky ● 1 part sweet vermouth

2 parts cherry brandy ● 2 parts lemon juice

Shake, pour into a tall glass over ice cubes and decorate with a slice of lemon.

SINGAPORE SLING

See *Classics* page 37

SUNSHINE NO. 5

1 part white rum ● 1 part dry vermouth

2 dashes cherry brandy ● 1 barspoon lemon juice

Shake.

VANDERBILT

1 part brandy ● 2 parts cherry brandy

2 dashes Angostura bitters ● 2 dashes sugar syrup

Stir and decorate with a twist of lemon and a cherry. An American version of this recipe calls for 2 parts brandy.

VODKA GILROY

1 part vodka ● 1 part lemon juice ● 1 part cherry brandy

3 barspoons dry vermouth ● 1 dash orange bitters

Shake.

WEDDING BELLES

2 parts gin ● 2 parts sweet vermouth ● 1 part cherry brandy

1 part orange juice ● 1 dash bitters per drink

Shake.

WHISPERING GAL

1 part whisky ● 1 part dry vermouth

1 part sweet vermouth ● 1 dash cherry brandy

Shake.

Apple Beauties

This is among the best known of the fruit brandies, also known as *eaux-de-vie*. Unlike liqueurs, which are made by flavouring a brandy base, these are distilled from the fermented mash of the fruit, as cognac is distilled from fermented grape juice. They range from rough, farmhouse brews to fine brandies. In the states of New England the brandies distilled from the mash of cider apples are known as applejack.

The best apple brandy of all is generally reckoned to be the Calvados produced in the region of Normandy of the same name and the finest Calvados comes from the *pays d'Auge* in the extreme east of the region. The best *pays d'Auge* Calvados enjoys, at least in its own region, the same prestige as the finest cognacs; the less prestigious local marques are often drunk from a small brandy snifter with a knob of sugar in the bottom.

	Dry Vermouth	Sweet Vermouth	Sherry/Port	Aperitif	Extras
Gin	Peppin the Inspired	Jules Verne So-So-Oh!	The Spaniard		Royal Smile Star Daisy
Vodka	Tsar Star White Prince		Russian Apple Brandy	Lunchtime	Scarlet Apple
Rum		Kicker			Liberty
Brandy	Pepino	Corpse Reviver Jersey Lightning	Lusatian Delicious		Depth Bomb
Extras	Klondike Woodstock	Remarkable		Bentley	Apple Brandy Sour Jack in the Box Jack Rose

APPLE BRANDY SOUR

1 large measure Calvados ● juice of $\frac{1}{2}$ lemon

$\frac{1}{2}$ barspoon powdered sugar

Shake and strain into a cocktail glass or small whisky tumbler.

BENTLEY

1 part apple brandy ● 1 part Dubonnet

Stir.

CORPSE REVIVER

See *Classics* page 33

DEPTH BOMB

1 part brandy ● 1 part apple brandy

2 dashes grenadine per drink ● 1 dash lemon juice per drink

Shake.

JACK IN THE BOX

3 parts apple brandy ● 2 parts pineapple juice

1 part lime juice ● 1 dash bitters per drink

Shake.

JACK ROSE

Something of a classic for which you will find many variants. Try this one, and substitute lime juice for the lemon if you have it.

5 parts apple brandy ● 2 parts lemon juice ● 1 part grenadine

---
Shake well.

JERSEY LIGHTNING

Once the name for American farmers' home-brew apple brandy, **Jersey Lightning** has graduated to a Savoy cocktail recipe.

2 parts brandy ● 1 part sweet vermouth

1 part apple brandy ● 1 dash Angostura bitters per drink

Shake.

JULES VERNE

3 parts gin ● 2 parts apple brandy ● 1 part sweet vermouth

2 barspoons lemon juice per drink ● 1 dash grenadine per drink

---
Shake.

KICKER

2 parts white rum ● 2 dashes sweet vermouth ● 1 part apple brandy

Stir. This cocktail is sometimes known as **Bolero**.

KLONDIKE WOODSTOCK

1 part dry vermouth ● 2 parts apple brandy ● 1 dash bitters

Shake.

LIBERTY

1 part white rum ● 2 parts apple brandy ● 1 dash sugar syrup

Shake.

LUNCHTIME

1 part vodka ● 1 part apple brandy

1 part Dubonnet ● 1 dash bitters

Shake.

LUSATIAN DELICIOUS

2 parts brandy ● 1 part apple brandy ● 2 parts port

Shake.

PEPINO

1 part brandy ● 1 part dry vermouth

1 part apple brandy ● 1 part orange juice

Stir.

PEPPIN THE INSPIRED

1 part gin ● 1 part dry vermouth

1 part apple brandy ● 1 part orange juice

Shake.

REMARKABLE

1 part Calvados ● 3 parts sweet vermouth ● 1 dash bitters per drink

---

Stir.

ROYAL SMILE

2 parts gin ● 1 part apple brandy

3 dashes lemon juice ● 2 dashes grenadine

Shake well.

RUSSIAN APPLE BRANDY

1 part vodka ● 1 part port ● 1 part apple brandy

Shake.

SCARLET APPLE

1 part vodka ● 1 dash apple brandy ● 1 part apple juice

2 barspoons lemon juice ● 1 barspoon grenadine

Shake.

SO-SO-OH!

2 parts gin ● 2 parts sweet vermouth

1 part apple brandy ● 1 part grenadine

Shake.

THE SPANIARD

2 parts gin ● 1 part apple brandy ● 2 parts sherry

1 part orange juice ● 2 dashes bitters

Shake.

STAR DAISY

1 part gin ● 1 part apple brandy ● 1 barspoon grenadine

2 dashes sugar syrup ● 2 barspoons lemon juice

Shake.

TSAR STAR

1 part vodka ● 1 dash sweet vermouth ● 1 dash dry vermouth

1 part apple brandy ● 1 barspoon grenadine

Shake.

WHITE PRINCE

1 part vodka ● 1 part dry vermouth ● 1 part apple brandy

Stir.

Monastic Mysteries

All the many modern liqueurs have evolved from the medicinal alcoholic preparations of the Middle Ages. The oldest surviving recipe and, in the opinion of many, still the best is that prepared since the early sixteenth century at the Benedictine Abbey of Fécamp, in Normandy. Composed to a secret formula of brandy, herbs and a sweetening agent, Benedictine bottles still bear the legend DOM, the initial letters of the Latin *Deo Optimo Maximo*— 'To God, Most Good, Most Great'.

The herb garden was a vital working tool for the medieval monastic infirmary and Fécamp was not alone in exploiting its resources to produce an elixir which, if curative, was also undoubtedly delicious. About a century later, the Carthusian monks at the Grande Chartreuse or Charterhouse Monastery near Grenoble developed a rival recipe. It is said to comprise no fewer than 130 herbs and spices and comes in two forms—Green Chartreuse, much the stronger, drier and more aromatic, and the sweeter Yellow Chartreuse.

All liqueurs are compounded on the same principle of a spirit base, flavouring agents such as herbs, flowers, fruits, and some form of sweetener, now usually sugar syrup but in former times often honey. However, in the opinion of connoisseurs none surpass this triad of ancient monastic mysteries.

BENEDICTINE

BOBBY BURNS

1 part whisky ● 1 part sweet vermouth

1 barspoon Benedictine per drink

Stir and add a twist of lemon peel. You can make this as a **Rob Roy** with 2 parts whisky to 1 part vermouth. Some American recipes substitute Drambuie for the Benedictine.

CABARET

2 parts gin ● 1 part dry vermouth

1 barspoon Benedictine ● 1 dash bitters

Stir and serve with a cherry. An alternative recipe substitutes an aperitif for the vermouth and a dash of absinthe for the Benedictine.

HONEYMOON

2 parts apple brandy ● 1 barspoon curacao per drink

1 part Benedictine ● 1 part lemon or lime juice

Shake. Many versions give equal measures of apple brandy and Benedictine, but I prefer the above.

HONOLULU

1 part gin ● 1 part maraschino ● 1 part Benedictine

Stir.

MERRY WIDOW

1 part gin ● 1 part dry vermouth ● 1 dash Pernod per drink

2 dashes Benedictine per drink ● 1 dash bitters or 2 dashes orange

bitters per drink

Shake and add a twist of lemon peel.

ROLLS-ROYCE

2 parts gin ● 1 part dry vermouth

1 part sweet vermouth ● 1 dash Benedictine per drink

Stir. The name **Rolls-Royce** is also given to a cocktail of equal parts of brandy, curacao and orange juice.

CHARTREUSE

ALASKA

3 parts gin ● 1 part yellow Chatreuse

Shake. An American version calls for 2:1 gin to Chartreuse and a liberal dash of orange bitters.

BIJOU

1 part gin ● 1 part green Chartreuse ● 1 part sweet vermouth

2 dashes orange bitters

Stir, then add a cherry or olive and twist a zest of lemon over the drink. According to an older generation, Plymouth is the correct gin for a **Bijou** cocktail.

CHAMPS-ELYSEES

3 parts brandy ● 1 part yellow Chartreuse

1 part lemon juice ● 1 dash Angostura bitters per drink

Shake. For those with a sweet tooth, reduce the proportions of gin to Chartreuse to 2:1 and add a dash of sugar syrup.

CHOCOLATE

1 barspoon brandy per drink • 1 part yellow Chartreuse

3 parts port • 1 egg yolk per drink

1 barspoon grated bitter chocolate per drink

Shake. There are a number of variations on this theme and you may omit brandy or chocolate or both according to your preferences.

EVERYBODY'S IRISH

2 ounces Irish whiskey • 1 barspoon green crème de menthe

1 barspoon green Chartreuse • 1 dash bitters

Stir and serve with a green olive. A variant, sometimes known as **St. Patrick's Day**, calls for equal quantities of the three main ingredients.

GOLDEN SLIPPER

1 part apricot brandy • 1 part yellow Chartreuse • 1 egg yolk

1 dash bitters (optional)

Shake. One variant substitutes Vantziger Goldwasser for the apricot brandy. Another calls for the liqueur ingredients to be stirred and the unbroken egg yolk floated on top.

SAND MARTIN

1 part gin • 1 part sweet vermouth

1 barspoon green Chartreuse per drink

Stir—even if some authorities say shake.

SPRING FEELING

2 parts gin • 1 part green Chartreuse • 1 part lemon juice

Shake.

WIDOW'S KISS

2 parts brandy ● 1 part Benedictine

1 part yellow Chartreuse ● 1 dash bitters per drink

Shake. According to some, widows prefer apple brandy.

XANTHIA

1 part gin ● 1 part cherry brandy ● 1 part yellow Chartreuse

Stir.

YELLOW PARROT

1 part apricot brandy ● 1 part yellow Chartreuse

1 part absinthe

Shake. Pastis or anisette are preferred to Pernod.

Galliano & Friends

This golden herbal liqueur, in its characteristic tapering, fluted bottle, is named after Major Galliano, an Italian military hero and is made at Livorno. It is, of course, an essential ingredient of that classic cocktail, the **Harvey Wallbanger** (see p. 35), but it has become increasingly popular in the USA and Britain and is now found in an increasing number of cocktail recipes. The following selection represents some of the best.

ADD ONE

1 part gin ● 1 part sweet vermouth ● 1 barspoon Dubonnet

1 part Galliano ● 1 dash bitters

Stir. Serve with a cherry.

BOSSA NOVA

2 parts white rum ● 1 part Galliano

2 parts pineapple juice ● 1 barspoon lime juice per drink

Shake.

GOLDEN CADILLAC

1 part crème de cacao ● 1 part Galliano ● 1 part cream

Shake or blend with crushed ice. Serve in a saucer champagne glass.

GOLDEN DREAM

1 part curacao ● 1 part Galliano

3 barspoons orange juice ● 1 part cream

Shake and decorate with a slice of orange and a cherry.

GOLD MEDAL

1 part brandy ● 1 part apricot brandy ● 1 part Galliano

1 egg white per two drinks ● 1 dash orange juice

Shake. Pour the orange juice over ice cubes in a tumbler and strain into the glass. Decorate with a wheel slice of orange.

MORESCO

2 parts gin ● 1 barspoon cherry brandy per drink

1 part Galliano ● 1 part grapefruit juice

Shake.

PICADOR

2 parts whisky ● 1 part dry vermouth ● 1 part Galliano

Stir.

Recommended Permutations

In a way, of course, all cocktails are permutations on the eternal theme of alcohol. But, as you will have learnt from the charts, some go better together than others. In this chapter there are a few recipes which suggest ideas using liqueurs of different flavours together. Apple and orange are natural partners, as any one who has eaten a Cox's Orange Pippin will know. But apples and apricots, too, can produce many delicious flavours, while cherry and orange are surprisingly good companions.

The chapter closes with some recipes for sloe gin cocktails.

ANGEL FACE

2 parts gin ● 1 part apricot brandy ● 1 part apple brandy

Shake. Some recommend equal parts of the three ingredients, though this makes too sweet a drink for my taste.

CALVADOS

2 parts apple brandy ● 1 part curacao or Cointreau

2 parts orange juice ● 1 dash Angostura bitters per drink

Shake. If you use Cointreau and the best quality Calvados in this recipe it is worth using orange bitters, and in that case add 1 barspoon to each drink.

CHERRY BLOSSOM

3 parts brandy ● 2 parts cherry brandy

1 barspoon curacao per drink ● 1 barspoon grenadine per drink

1 barspoon lemon juice per drink

Shake and serve with a cherry. Moisten the rim of the glass with maraschino cherry liquor and dip in castor sugar for a pretty and tasty effect. The classic version calls for good quality Kirsch in place of the cherry brandy. In this case, reverse the proportions of brandy and Kirsch.

CLASSIC

3 parts brandy ● 1 part maraschino

1 part curacao ● 1 part lemon juice

Shake. Dip the rim of the glass in lemon juice and frost with castor sugar. Add a twist of lemon.

RUSTY NAIL

2 parts whisky ● 1 part Drambuie

Stir and serve on the rocks, if desired.

SLOE GIN

BLACKTHORN

2 parts sloe gin ● 1 part sweet vermouth

Stir. Serve with a twist of lemon. For a **Sweet and Slow**, leave out the lemon twist but add a dash of orange bitters.

ECLIPSE

1 part gin ● 2 parts sloe gin ● 1 barspoon grenadine

Place an olive in the cocktail glass and pour over the grenadine. Stir the gin and sloe gin on ice and pour on to the grenadine and olive taking care not to mix.

SLOE GIN COCKTAIL

2 parts sloe gin ● 1 part dry vermouth

1 dash sweet vermouth ● 1 dash orange bitters

Stir.

Champagne Special

The most famous of all wines is made from the grapes grown in the gravelly soil of the Champagne region of France. The method, *champenois*, which produces the bubbles, was developed in the early eighteenth century and the wine soon became the height of fashion. In Vienna, the Imperial Minister Prince Kaunitz considered himself something of an expert on the correct way to pour champagne and entertained a banquet in the Schönbrunn Palace with a demonstration. 'Unfortunately,' we are told, 'he missed the calculation of his parabola and poured the wine into his upturned sleeve as well as into his waistcoat.'

Since that time many other wine-growing areas have adapted similar methods. German *Sekt* is outstanding, though it tends to be sweet as do the Italian *spumante* wines. Spanish *cava* is becoming increasingly popular and there are also American versions. France, in fact, produces a whole range of other sparkling wines, not so fine—or so expensive—as good champagne but often very good and it is perfectly sensible to use them in the recipes in this section especially as the quality of a fine champagne is likely to be submerged by the other contending flavours.

Do not forget to chill your champagne.

CHAMPAGNE COCKTAIL

1 barspoon cognac ● 1 dash Angostura bitters

1 lump sugar ● champagne

Place the sugar lump in a champagne glass and soak with two or three dashes of bitters. Add the brandy at this stage for the special effect and top up with champagne. I like my champagne cocktails unadorned but some decorate with a slice of orange and a cherry. Variants on this basic recipe substitute other liquor for the brandy. In every case just a barspoon is sufficient to give the desired.

For **Fizzy Orange** use curacao; for **Awake and Rise My Love** use green crème de menthe; for **Banana Beauty** one barspoon crème de banane and a dash of white rum; for **Cherry Special** add a barspoon of cherry brandy and a dash of curacao; for the **Alphonse** use a barspoon of Dubonnet and add, if you wish, a twist of lemon peel. For **Champagne Napoleon** pour two barspoons of Mandarine Napoleon and one of orange juice over the sugar lump and bitters and top up with the champagne.

In all these cases you may increase the quantity of the flavouring agent if you wish and, within reason, you will find any fruit brandy or liqueur of your taste worth experimenting with.

AMBROSIA

3 barspoons brandy ● 3 barspoons apple brandy

1 dash curacao ● 2 barspoons lemon juice ● champagne

Shake, pour over ice cubes in a tall glass and top up with iced champagne. Add a twist of orange peel.

APPLE SUPERB

This is a champagne cocktail in which the brandy is replaced with two barspoons of apple brandy, ideally the best Calvados. For **Cider Superb** follow the same method but substitute a good, dry pomagne cider for the champagne.

BELLINI

2 parts champagne ● 1 part peach juice

If the name had not been given to another drink this could equally well be called 'Ambrosia'. Fill a champagne glass about one third full with peach juice and top up with champagne.

BLACK VELVET

1 part Guinness ● 1 part champagne

Taking your best beer tankards, pour in the equal quantities of chilled Guinness and champagne—carefully and in that order, if you do not want to risk the 'Kaunitz' effect. If you are giving a **Black Velvet** party few, if any, of your guests will object to find their glasses topped up from a large jug well filled with the prepared mixture. It may not be strictly kosher but it does save time and helps you circulate.

BUCK'S FIZZ

2 parts champagne ● 1 part orange juice

Fill a champagne glass about one third full with fresh orange juice and top up with champagne. Again, if any purist objects to having a top up from a jug of the mixture, move on to the next glass.

FRENCH '75

1 part gin ● 1 part lemon juice
2 dashes sugar syrup ● 4 parts champagne

Some recipes call for more gin than lemon juice; in any case do not use more than 1 ounce of either. Shake with the sugar and strain into a champagne glass then top up with champagne.

KIR ROYALE

1 barspoon crème de cassis ● champagne

Pour a small barspoonful of crème de cassis into an eight-ounce wine glass and top up with champagne.

MONTE CARLO IMPERIAL

2 parts gin ● 1 part white crème de menthe
1 part lemon juice ● 3 parts champagne

Shake and strain over ice cubes in a tall glass and top up with champagne. If you have only green crème de menthe, use it.

PIPPIN COLD PUNCH

A good dry Pomagne cider substituted for the champagne in all the recipes in this section makes an enjoyable—and economical—drink. **Pippin Cold Punch** specifically calls for it.

½ pint Calvados ● 4 ounces Cointreau ● 4 bottles Pomagne cider

1 pint orange juice or cold tea ● oranges, apples

Rough cut two oranges and steep in the Calvados and Cointreau for three or four hours. Put a large block of ice into a punch bowl, strain the spirit over it, add the orange juice or tea and then the Pomagne. Decorate with slices of apples and orange.

TT SPECIAL

1 part lemon juice ● 1 part orange juice ● 1 part pineapple juice

1 part champagne

Shake on ice in these proportions or to taste, then add the champagne. If sparkling grape juice is substituted for the champagne, this makes an excellent non-alcoholic drink.

VALENCIA

2 parts apricot brandy ● 1 part orange juice

1 dash Angostura bitters ● 3 parts champagne

Shake, strain and top up with champagne. Orange bitters really are preferable here—use a small barspoonful for each drink.

Tequila Treats

The Mexican spirit tequila won something of an early reputation in the USA smuggled in as a substitute for gin during Prohibition days. It was not until the Seventies that it appeared in Britain and it has become increasingly popular ever since. It is distilled from the fermented sap and heart pulp of a cactus-like plant known in Mexico as the maguey, or blue mezcal. It comes in two styles—*Blanco* (white or silver) and Extra or *Anejo* which is matured in oak giving it a golden colour and somewhat mellower taste. The finest tequila is reckoned to come from the region round the village of the same name.

To drink it neat in the Mexican way you take a wedge of lemon in your left hand, shake a dash of salt on the back of the same hand and take up the tequila glass in the right. Lick the salt, squeeze a stream of lemon juice on to the tongue and then take a pull at the drink. If the tequila is very cold and the sun as hot as possible the 'Mexican Itch', as it is sometimes irreverently called, can be, even for the uninitiated, a tolerable substitute for drinking.

As a cocktail ingredient, however, tequila works excellently and the **Margarita**, listed in the classic section of this book, is a well-established favourite. Tequila enthusiasts will no doubt be outraged by the tone of these remarks—I can only hope they will approve my selection of tequila-based recipes.

BUTLER'S MEXICAN

2 parts tequila ● 1 part orange juice

1 part lemon juice ● 1 barspoon sugar syrup or grenadine

Shake.

EASY GLOW

1 part vodka ● 1 part gin ● 1 part tequila

1 barspoon grenadine ● orange juice

Shake all but the orange juice. Pour over ice in a tall glass and top up with the orange juice. Decorate with a slice of orange and a cherry.

MEXICAN

3 parts tequila ● 2 parts pineapple juice

1 part lemon or lime juice ● 2 dashes grenadine

Shake.

MONTEZUMA

3 parts tequila ● 2 parts sweet sherry

1 egg yolk ● $\frac{1}{2}$ cup crushed ice

Blend at low speed in an electric blender and serve in a saucer champagne glass.

ROBERTA

2 parts tequila ● 1 part dry vermouth

1 part sweet vermouth ● 1 part Campari

Pour over ice in a tumbler and stir. Add lemon peel.

SILK STOCKINGS

3 parts tequila ● 1 part crème de cacao ● 1 part cream

1 dash grenadine per drink ● cinnamon powder

Blend with crushed ice. Serve sprinkled with cinnamon in a wine glass, with a straw. Essentially, this is a variant of **Toreador** which has the same ingredients but for the grenadine: shake the ingredients; pour into a cocktail glass, top with whipped cream and sprinkle lightly with flakes of drinking chocolate.

TEQUILA SUNRISE

1 part tequila ● 2 parts orange juice ● 1 barspoon grenadine

Carefully pour the grenadine into the bottom of a chilled tall glass. Stir the tequila and orange juice on ice in a mixing glass and strain into the glass so that it splashes on to the grenadine. Add ice cubes.

VIVA VILLA

3 parts tequila ● 1 part lime juice

1 barspoon sugar syrup per drink ● a pinch of salt

Shake the ingredients with ice and strain into a tall ice-filled glass.

Bourbon & Associates

There are numerous variations and refinements of American whiskey but all tend to be somewhat sweeter and heavier than Scotch. Bourbon is the best known of the spirits distilled from corn grain and the best comes from Kentucky. The other main group of American whiskeys are distilled from rye, the traditional centres of production being Maryland and Pennsylvania. The Canadian whiskeys are blended and usually distilled from rye, corn and barley and are lighter than American whiskey. Irish whiskey, like Scotch, is a blend of malted barley and grain spirits but the difference in flavour is the result of different methods of production.

ALGONQUIN

3 parts rye whiskey ● 2 parts dry vermouth

1 part pineapple juice

Shake.

CANADIAN CHERRY

3 parts Canadian whiskey ● 1 part cherry brandy

2 barspoons lemon juice per drink ● 2 barspoons orange juice per drink

Shake and pour over ice cubes in a tall glass.

THE MANHATTAN

2 parts rye whiskey ● 1 part sweet vermouth

1 dash Angostura bitters

Stir and serve with a cherry. This may be called the **Original Manhattan** though you will find many variations in the proportions. This is sometimes also called the **Sweet Manhattan**. The **Dry Manhattan** substitutes dry vermouth for the sweet and is served with a twist of lemon peel. The **Medium**, sometimes called the **Perfect Manhattan**, is made of rye, sweet and dry vermouth, usually in proportions of 4:1:1, and is served with both a twist of lemon peel and a cherry.

MILLIONAIRE RYE

3 parts rye whiskey ● 1 part curacao

1 dash grenadine per drink ● 1 egg white per 2 drinks

Shake.

THE MINT JULEP

2 ounces bourbon whiskey ● mint

2 barspoons sugar syrup per drink

This is the classic drink of the Southern States. To make it well you will need large tall glasses, chilled as much as possible and young fresh sprigs of mint.

For each drink put 2 barspoons of sugar syrup and half a dozen or more mint leaves into the mixing glass. Stir for some minutes bruising but not crushing the mint leaves then add enough bourbon to allow 2 ounces per drink. Stir again. Now take the glasses from the fridge and fill with finely crushed ice (the *cognoscenti* wrap the glasses in a dry towel to avoid contact with the warm hand). Pour the ingredients of the mixing jug into the ice-filled glasses and stir again until they are heavily frosted. Decorate with sugar-frosted mint leaves and straws.

NEW YORK

2 ounces rye whiskey ● 1 barspoon grenadine

juice of 1 lime or ½ lemon ● 1 dash sugar syrup

Shake and add a twist of lemon peel. Bourbon whiskey can be used instead.

THE OLD FASHIONED

2 ounces rye whiskey ● 1 or 2 barspoons sugar syrup

1 or 2 dashes bitters

Muddle the sugar syrup, bitters and a little of the whiskey in the bottom of a small whisky tumbler or old-fashioned glass. Drop in two or three cubes of ice and fill with whiskey. Decorate with a cherry on a stick and a slice of orange or lemon and serve with a stirrer.

SHAMROCK

3 parts Irish whiskey ● 1 part dry vermouth

1 barspoon crème de menthe (green) per drink ● 1 dash green

Chartreuse per drink

Stir and serve with an olive. Alternatively, try equal parts of whiskey and vermouth.

SOUL KISS

1 part Bourbon whiskey ● 1 part dry vermouth

2 barspoons Dubonnet ● 2 barspoons orange juice

Shake. This is a whiskey variant of an earlier **Soul Kiss** recipe of equal parts dry and sweet vermouth and Dubonnet shaken with 1 or 2 barspoons of orange juice.

TEMPTATION

2 ounces rye whiskey ● 1 barspoon Cointreau ● 1 barspoon Dubonnet

2 dashes Pernod

Shake. Add a twist each of orange and lemon peel.

TNT

1 part rye whiskey ● 1 part Pernod

Shake.

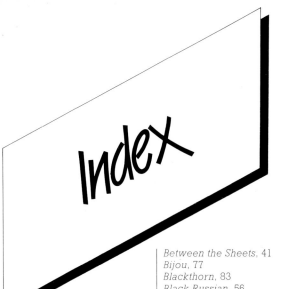

Index